Baby Carnivores

![Crabtree logo]
Bobbie Kalman
Crabtree Publishing Company
www.crabtreebooks.com

It's fun to learn about Baby Animals

Created by Bobbie Kalman

For Alice Hope King,
with lots of love from your Auntie Sam
You are so cute, I could eat you up!

**Author and
Editor-in-Chief**
Bobbie Kalman

Editors
Kathy Middleton
Crystal Sikkens

Design
Bobbie Kalman
Katherine Berti
Samantha Crabtree
(logo and front cover)

Photo research
Bobbie Kalman

Print and production coordinator
Katherine Berti

Prepress technician
Katherine Berti

Photographs
BigStockPhoto: pages 5, 24 (nursing)
All other images by Shutterstock

Library and Archives Canada Cataloguing in Publication

Kalman, Bobbie
      Baby carnivores / Bobbie Kalman.

(It's fun to learn about baby animals)
Includes index.
Issued also in electronic formats.
ISBN 978-0-7787-1010-3 (bound).--ISBN 978-0-7787-1015-8 (pbk.)

      1. Carnivora--Infancy--Juvenile literature. I. Title. II. Series:
It's fun to learn about baby animals

QL737.C2K33 2013   j599.713'92   C2012-907327-X

Library of Congress Cataloging-in-Publication Data

CIP available at Library of Congress

Crabtree Publishing Company

www.crabtreebooks.com   1-800-387-7650

Printed in Hong Kong/012013/BK20121102

Published in Canada
Crabtree Publishing
616 Welland Ave.
St. Catharines, Ontario
L2M 5V6

Published in the United States
Crabtree Publishing
PMB 59051
350 Fifth Avenue, 59th Floor
New York, New York 10118

Published in the United Kingdom
Crabtree Publishing
Maritime House
Basin Road North, Hove
BN41 1WR

Published in Australia
Crabtree Publishing
3 Charles Street
Coburg North
VIC, 3058

What is in this book?

What is a carnivore?

Animals eat different kinds of foods. Some animals eat mainly plants. Some eat other animals. Animals that eat mainly other animals are called **carnivores**. Carnivore means "meat-eater." Carnivores can be birds, snakes, and fish, but the carnivores in this book belong to a group of **mammals** called **carnivora**. Mammals are animals that have hair or fur on their bodies. Mammals that belong to the carnivora group also have sharp teeth and long, pointed claws.

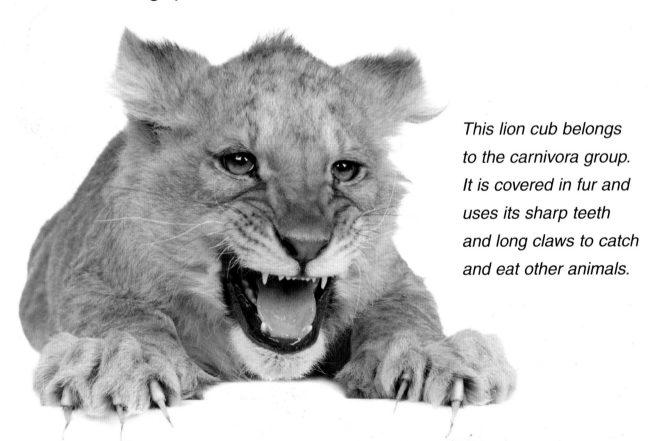

This lion cub belongs to the carnivora group. It is covered in fur and uses its sharp teeth and long claws to catch and eat other animals.

From milk to meat

Mammal babies drink milk that is made in the bodies of their mothers. Drinking mother's milk is called **nursing**. Mammal babies nurse soon after they are born. As the babies grow, they nurse less often and start eating the foods their parents eat.

*These fox babies, called **kits**, are nursing. Their mother will soon teach them how to find food. What kinds of foods do foxes eat? Turn to page 15 to find out.*

Carnivora families

There are thirteen carnivora families and 270 different **species**, or types, of carnivora animals. Learn more about these families and animals in this book.

This baby leopard belongs to the cat family. Lions, tigers, cheetahs, cougars, lynx, and pet cats are some of the cats that belong to this family (see pages 16–17).

wolf pup

Wolves, coyotes, foxes, jackals, and pet dogs belong to the dog family (see pages 14–15).

*Sea lions and seals are animals called **pinnipeds**. Sea lions have ear flaps, but seals do not (see page 23).*

This baby ferret belongs to the weasel family, along with wolverines, badgers, and otters (see page 18).

Raccoons and coatis make up another carnivora family. These animals eat plants as well as meat (see page 19).

This polar bear cub is part of the bear family. It eats only meat, but some other bears eat plants, too (see page 22).

These young meerkats belong to the mongoose family (see pages 20–21).

7

Mammal bodies

Mammals have a group of bones, called a **backbone**, in the middle of their backs. Animals with backbones are called **vertebrates**. Mammals also have **limbs**. A limb can be an arm, leg, or flipper. Mammals use their limbs to walk, run, climb, or swim.

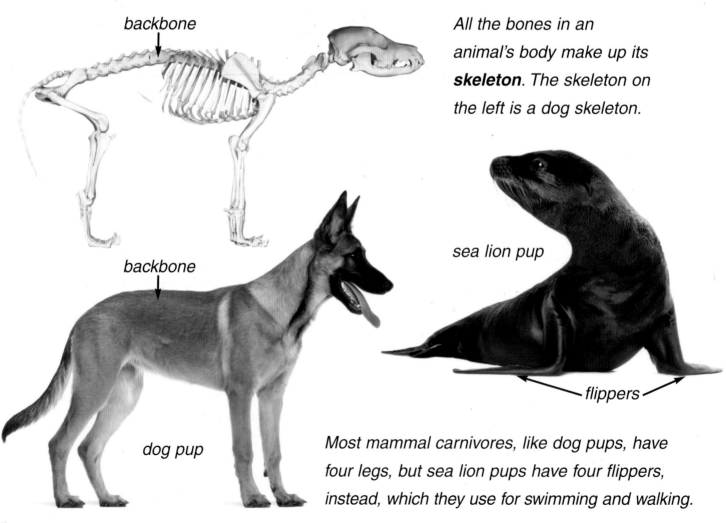

backbone

All the bones in an animal's body make up its skeleton. The skeleton on the left is a dog skeleton.

backbone

sea lion pup

dog pup

flippers

Most mammal carnivores, like dog pups, have four legs, but sea lion pups have four flippers, instead, which they use for swimming and walking.

Keeping warm

Mammals are **warm-blooded**. The body temperature of warm-blooded animals stays about the same in both warm and cold places. Some mammals have thick fur coats that keep them warm in cold weather.

*This polar bear cub has a thick layer of **blubber**, or fat, under its skin, as well as two layers of warm fur.*

Carnivore teeth

The teeth at the front of a carnivora mammal's mouth are sharp and pointed. Four of the teeth, called **canines**, are longer than the others. The teeth at the back of the mouth are also sharp and pointed.

This lion has ridges on the roof of its mouth and on its tongue. Ridges help the lion shred its food.

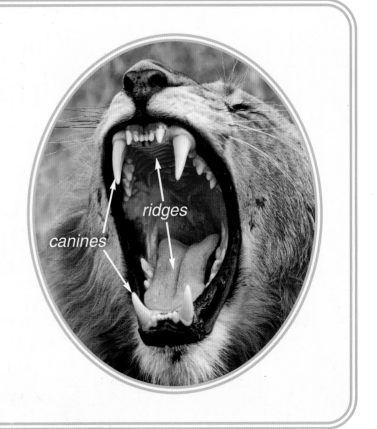

canines

ridges

Where do they live?

Carnivores live all over the world in different **habitats**, or natural places. Some live in forests, and some live on **savannas**. Savannas are large grassy areas with a few trees. Carnivores also live in **deserts**, which are dry areas that get very little rain. There are also carnivores that live in water habitats such as oceans and rivers. Pet dogs and cats are carnivores that live with people.

This cheetah mother and her five cubs live on the savanna in Africa. Savannas are hot and dry for most of the year. Cheetahs are wild cats that hunt animals such as zebras and antelopes.

These coyote pups live in a forest where many trees and other plants grow.

This meerkat family lives in a hot, dry desert in Africa.

Polar bears live in a cold place in the north of Earth, called the Arctic. Part of the Arctic is frozen ocean, and part is land. Polar bears spend time both on land and in the ocean.

Learning to be predators

This lion cub is practicing her hunting skills by gently biting her mother's neck.

Many carnivores are **predators**. Predators hunt other animals. The animals that predators hunt are called **prey**. Baby predators hunt with their mothers. Their mothers teach them how to catch prey in different ways.

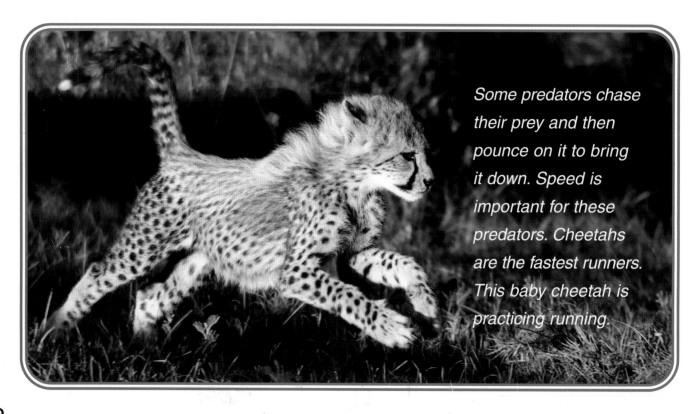

Some predators chase their prey and then pounce on it to bring it down. Speed is important for these predators. Cheetahs are the fastest runners. This baby cheetah is practicing running.

This lion mother is taking her cubs to eat part of the animal she has hunted. Soon, the cubs will also start hunting.

This brown bear mother is teaching her cub how to fish for salmon. Salmon are fish that swim up waterfalls, where brown bears wait to catch them.

salmon

pet puppy

The dog family

Wolves, foxes, coyotes, and jackals belong to the dog family. They are **wild dogs**. Wild dogs live in different parts of the world. Their homes are in **nature**, or in outdoor places not made by people. Pet dogs live with people.

Wolves are the biggest members of the dog family. They hunt large prey such as deer. This mother and pup live in a forest.

Coyotes hunt rabbits, squirrels, and other small prey. These coyote pups are not yet ready to hunt. Their mother feeds them.

This jackal mother is feeding her pup meat brought up from her stomach. Wolf and coyote mothers also feed their babies this way when they return from hunting.

One of these red fox kits is nursing, and another is looking for prey that may be hiding under the ground. Foxes hunt, but they also eat plants.

Cat carnivores

All wild cats are carnivores and predators. They live in many kinds of habitats. Lions, leopards, tigers, and jaguars are big cats. Tigers are the biggest cats. Most big cats, except snow leopards, can roar.

Tigers live near water in forests, grasslands, and on mountains.

Most jaguars have spots, but the spots are harder to see on black jaguars like this one.

Leopards can climb trees and run fast. They live in Africa and Asia. Like jaguars, some leopards are also black.

Lions live on savannas. This cub cannot roar yet, but it will soon roar loudly.

Smaller cats

Another group of cats includes cougars, cheetahs, lynx, and ocelots. These cats are smaller than the big cats. Pet cats are the smallest cats. None of these cats can roar.

Ocelots are small cats that live in rain forests and in areas with many bushes. They hunt rabbits and other small animals.

Cougars are medium-sized cats that are fierce predators. This cougar cub will soon hunt deer and moose.

Lynx are smaller than lions, tigers, and cougars. They live in forests.

Cheetahs are sometimes called big cats, but they cannot roar.

The weasel family

The weasel family has the most species of carnivora animals. It includes least weasels, ferrets, badgers, wolverines, and otters. Most of these animals live on land, but otters live mainly in water.

(left) The least weasel is the smallest member of this family. It is about the size of a rat.

This baby ferret does not live in the wild. Ferrets are often kept as pets.

This river otter mother and her pups spend time both in water and on land. They are larger than most other members of the weasel family.

The raccoon family

Raccoons and coatis belong to another carnivora family, but they are not strict carnivores. They hunt mice, birds, and frogs, but they also eat plants. These animals can climb trees easily, but they often look for food on the ground.

(right) Mother raccoons take care of their kits and teach them how to find food.

This mother and baby coati are looking for worms and insects to eat. They dig them up with their sharp claws. Most coatis live in warm places, such as rain forests, but some live on cold mountains.

The mongoose family

This baby dwarf mongoose and its mother live in a termite mound.

There are more than 37 species of mongooses. They live in habitats such as deserts, savannas, and forests. Mongooses eat rats, rabbits, lizards, snakes, and birds. They live in large family groups called **troops**, **packs**, or **clans**.

This yellow mongoose mother and her baby live on a savanna in Africa.

Working together

Meerkats belong to the mongoose family. They work together to dig **burrows**, or underground homes. Meerkats have sharp claws for digging. To keep safe, groups of meerkats take turns watching for predators, such as jackals and eagles, while others look for food.

Meerkats often dig burrows together with yellow mongooses, like the mother and baby on the opposite page. This baby meerkat is about to go into its burrow home.

Baby bears

There are eight species of bears, and they all belong to the carnivora family. Most bears, however, are **omnivores**—not carnivores. Omnivores eat both plants and animals. The polar bear is the only true carnivore. It hunts and eats other animals.

Brown bears like to eat fish, but they also eat all kinds of plants.

Polar bears are predators that hunt and eat seals. The bears wait near a hole in the ice for a seal to come up for air. They then grab the seal and drag it onto the ice.

Seals and sea lions

Seals and sea lions live in oceans. They are animals called pinnipeds. Sea lions have ear flaps and can walk on land. Seals do not have ear flaps. They can swim well in water, but they do not move easily on land. Both seals and sea lions have thick layers of blubber, and both eat fish, squid, and crabs.

sea lion pup

This harp seal pup lives in the Arctic. It was just born. Its mother has gone to find fish to eat in the ocean. She will be back soon so her pup can nurse.

Words to Know and Index

bear family
pages 7, 9, 11, 13, 22

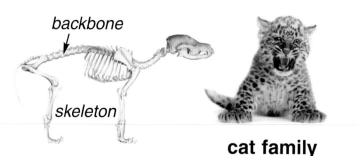
backbone
skeleton

bodies
pages 4, 5, 8–9

cat family
pages 6, 10, 16–17

dog family
pages 6, 14–15

habitats (homes)
pages 10–11, 16, 20, 21

mongoose family
pages 7, 20–21

nursing
pages 5, 15, 23

raccoon family
pages 7, 19

sea lions (seals)
pages 6, 8, 23

weasel family
pages 7, 18